Mounted police

Author: Mattern, Joanne
Reading Level; 2.4
Point Value: 0.5
ACCELERATED READER 88

READING POWER

Working Together

Mounted Police

Joanne Mattern

The Rosen Publishing Group's
PowerKids Press™
New York

Published in 2002 by The Rosen Publishing Group, Inc.
29 East 21st Street, New York, NY 10010

First Edition

Book Design: Laura Stein

Photo Credits: Cindy Reiman

Thanks to Captain Ron Shindel, Officer Kelly Balsam, the New York City Police Department Mounted Unit, the Office of the Deputy Commissioner of Public Information, and Selvaggi the horse

Mattern, Joanne, 1963–
Mounted police / by Joanne Mattern.
   p. cm. — (Working together)
ISBN 0-8239-5981-3
1. Mounted police—Juvenile literature. 2. Police horses—Juvenile literature. [1. Mounted police. 2. Police horses. 3. Police. 4. Horses.] I. Title. II. Series.
HV7922 .M367 2001
363.2'32—dc21

                                        2001001121

Manufactured in the United States of America

Contents

Meet the Mounted Police   4

Training the Horse   6

Working on Horseback   8

Police to the Rescue   16

Glossary   22

Resources   23

Index   24

Word Count   24

Note   24

Meet the Mounted Police

Police officers who work on horseback are called mounted police. These officers and their horses work together to help people and to fight crime.

Training the Horse

The horses that work with the mounted police need special training. The horses are trained to listen to the officer.

The horses also learn how to stay calm when there is a lot of noise.

Working on Horseback

The police officer arrives at the stable early in the morning.

The officer gets her horse ready to ride.

A mounted police officer and her horse use a lot of gear to do their jobs.

Helmet

Uniform

Reins

Saddle

Nightstick

Riding Boots

11

Today, the officer is riding through the park. Sitting high on a horse helps the officer see all around.

The officer sees a young boy crying. She rides over to help.

Police to the Rescue

The boy is lost in the park. He can't find his parents.

The officer uses her radio to call the police station. She asks if anyone has reported a missing child.

The officer tells the boy that his parents are waiting for him at the station. A police car will take the boy back to his parents.

The officer and her horse go back to the stable. Together, they work hard to keep people safe.

POLICE

Glossary

gear (**gihr**) things needed to do a job

mounted (**mown**-tuhd) to be on a horse

reins (**raynz**) long straps that a rider uses to
  guide a horse

saddle (**sad**-l) a seat for the rider that is
  strapped onto the horse's back

stable (**stay**-buhl) a building where horses
  are kept

Resources

Books

Mounted Police
by Michael Green
Capstone Press (1998)

Animals Protecting Us
by Robert Snedden
Franklin Watts, Inc. (2000)

Web Site

http://www.geocities.com/heartland/
ranch/9922/

Index

C
crime, 4

G
gear, 10

P
police station, 17

R
radio, 17

S
stable, 8, 20

Word Count: 200

Note to Librarians, Teachers, and Parents

If reading is a challenge, Reading Power is a solution! Reading Power is perfect for readers who want high-interest subject matter at an accessible reading level. These fact-filled, photo-illustrated books are designed for readers who want straightforward vocabulary, engaging topics, and a manageable reading experience. With clear picture/text correspondence, leveled Reading Power books put the reader in charge. Now readers have the power to get the information they want and the skills they need in a user-friendly format.